WITHOUT PARADISE

poems by

Richard Hoffman

WITHOUT PARADISE

ISBN 1-891812-33-5
Library of Congress Catalog Number: 2002110716

Grateful acknowledgement is made to the editors of the following publications in which a number of these poems first appeared: *American Review, The Carleton Miscellany, Green House, HeART Quarterly, Sandscript, Shenandoah, South Dakota Review, Stuff, The Sun,* and *Swift River.*

Some poems have also been included in the following anthologies:

Eating the Menu: Contemporary American Poetry, ed. Bruce Edward Taylor. Dubuque. Kendall-Hunt Publishing.

The Uses of Poetry, ed. Agnes Stein. New York. Holt, Rinehart and Winston.

An Ear to the Ground: Contemporary U.S. Poetry, ed. Kathleen Aguero & Marie Harris. Athens, GA. University of Georgia Press.

Stubborn Light: The Best of The Sun, Volume III, Chapel Hill, NC. The Sun.

The Grolier Poetry Annual, 2000. Cambridge, MA. The Ellen LaForge Poetry Foundation.

Cover design by Kerrie Kemperman
Cover illustration by Bill Regan, *Passage,* photo-collage, 2001
Author Photo by Robert Aguero-Hoffman

Distributed by: Small Press Distribution
1-800-869-7553
www.spdbooks.org

Cedar Hill Publications
San Diego, California
cedarhill_bks@hotmail.com

for Kathi

Contents

The paradise of pre-ambivalent harmony is unattainable. But the experience of one's own truth and the post-ambivalent knowledge of it, make it possible to return to one's own world of feelings at an adult level — without paradise, but with the ability to mourn.

— Alice Miller

Elegy

for Michael Stephen Hoffman, 1957-1970

Being in us in his new life
is as strange for him
as it is for us to be here

at his grave today
with no one else's footprints in the snow
and only the trees that guided us:

let it not be winter there.

Roll Over

The alarm clock buzzes but I am
dreaming of a tall field in August,
locusts.

As if the field were on fire,
lots of other tiny insects pop and crack
from stalk to stalk.

Underground
there are people waiting for me,
but I am unaware of them now.

They think I am late.

Miss Martha On Winter

"...no, I don't like it.
The oaks around the house
knock nights and creak and keep
me up late worrying and thinking.
Hell on a body's nerves. Come
spring I feel a little better
usually — some worries, you know,
melt with the snow but
it's not just the money part.
The birds! The goldfinch come here
all peagreen and wait
for the forsythia and willows
to get yellow (they won't take
the breadcrumbs while I'm out there.
All these years and still
they're afraid! Like children.)
When will someone finally get
smart enough to not get old?
You think that's funny but you
don't believe you will. I didn't.
Smell the air. This time of year,
especially in the rain, you
smell all kinds of poor
dead creatures, thawing in the mud."

Vipassana

What part of me is it that wants this self,
destined, I know by now, to go the way
of the Tooth Fairy, the Easter Bunny, and God,
to stay and be real, instead

of wishing it Bon Voyage as it leaves
to join them there, at the North Pole,
freezing their asses off with Santa Claus?
And who is this now, asking questions?

And isn't that Admiral Whatsisname there
looking dumbly at the flag he's planted,
no feeling in his hands or feet anymore?
I remember when I was him too, poor bastard.

The Sloth

I live entirely for my own sake.
I once had friends, some money, plans, a love,
but what the hell, what difference does it make?

These days it doesn't pay to stay awake.
I've got what I need. I've got nothing to prove.
I live entirely for my own sake.

I was the best but couldn't catch a break.
So here I hang. I should be hanging in the Louvre!
But what the hell, what difference does it make?

Just thinking of work gives me a headache.
I like it here, a bit above it all; why move?
I live entirely for my own sake.

I've taken all the shit I'm gonna take.
So take your shining mottoes, squat, and shove.
But what the hell, what difference does it make?

Your lives, your loves, your work: they're fake.
You're all stuck in the same timekilling groove.
I live entirely for my own sake.
What the hell, what difference does it make?

Nude Descending A Prayer

Father Art, on earth, above those past
the hours of their deaths, thou Mother
under us for who knows how long now,
thy names be with me. Fruit of wills
repeatedly and variously done on earth,
who will pray for us? Sinners? I believe
in clay and constellations and what accidents
allow us to forgive ourselves again for being
in such debt, for owing bread, for being tempted
to make believe, to lie, to sleep forever. *Amen.*

Good Friday

He's gone
to find the animal
who tells the story
that destroys us;
he wants to interview
the angel with the teeth;

unearth
disfigured miniature
intaglios: clay
dolls of heroes, words
burnt into buried stones,
the molds for masks we

memorized
and wear for worship,
somber and nodding and
simpler than we know we are.
Look at the bloodless body
hanging from a rootless tree:

no wonder
in our fear we carve it,
paint it, sing of it, and
pray to believe that only one
unlike ourselves is sanctioned
to attempt such things.

Sweat

A man is mowing between the rows of headstones
on a little toy-like tractor. It's hot;
he wipes his face and underneath his cap.
The sun glares off the polished stones.

He hates it - the job, the heat, the flies;
he wanted to be something else.
The sweat on the back of his dark green shirt
could be a black, triangular insignia.

And with his shears, on his hands and knees,
trimming around the crosses, angels, urns,
crawling from stone to stone, he could be
grieving inconsolably for everyone.

Stories

for Robert James Hoffman, 1950-1972

I was lying on my belly
using my head
to shade the bright pages of an old book

next to me a tree
had broken over at its trunk the whole crown
deep in the river...

I was lying on my back
which didn't work
because the book weighed more than ever

and the tree said
Now that they nest in my branches I know fish
sing morning and evening

I am lying through my teeth
the story isn't true
He wasn't a tree there is no tree

and death says nothing
Now that it nests in my branches I know stories
alone have wings

I tell these,
cup them beating in my hands
and fling them into the air above the river...

1.

He shook the green package.
Why the gift was taken back
before he opened it was not his question.

He remembered the sound, the feel.
Was it something broken?
Or something to be assembled?

2.

we are told
that even after we have closed the eyes
we may be heard
so we are careful what we say

you never know
maybe it is best to say nothing

3.

In the fire, an envelope
furls, darkening,

behind the man
who, reading, slowly moves away

4.

The people
in the interval when all grew dark and quiet
all lay down.
You would see their bodies lying on the plain for miles.

Always an echo of singing woke them.
Always there were some who did not rise.

These the people would place in the ground
and cover them over,
these who were called in the night
to join their fathers in the song.

Dark Otherwise

Awake, memories come to you.
Asleep, you go to them:

an old woman, a prancing pony,
a priest, a powdered clown, a soldier,

others. They sit you on the floor
and dance around you. There is a baby

waving its hands in ways the dancers know
and follow, faster, faster; everybody

in their dream clothes, colors
where you look, dark otherwise.

You have no idea who they are.
The dance is not for you but for the child.

You are asleep, dreaming.
The child is radiant, pleased with you.

Lining-off The Field

My father handed me the flags and paid
out string from where he stood
at home, waving me deeper, waving me right
or left, "More left. A little less. Yes.
Good." Then with the string held high,
a wind-rolled arc
between us, I ran hard across
the outfield and we set the Left-field flag.

Suppose the string were one thread of a sail;
the way it would belly, filling
with assurance. Say that where he stood on it
it entered the ground
so if I pulled I'd pull forever, all of it —
the whole ball — one unbroken strand.
Or say I doubled back
to a snag in crabgrass or a patch of dandelion
too late and saw my father
chasing the end that got away from him.

Suppose the lines go on beyond the flags,
embracing houses, trees,
so many men and women, strangers
turning into friends or enemies, so many lovers,
towns, forests, lakes, rivers, stories
told and heard, forgotten or remembered,
understood or not. suppose the lines go on
because they do; imaginary, real.

A Parable For First Monday, January

Driving home from the warehouse,
little jazz on FM, the moon low
and full over the frozen reservoir,
a powder polishing the ice.

Suppose
those lights behind me, gaining,
were someone speeding to catch up
to tell me I'd forgotten something;

not this flatbed rattling past
with a load of empties.

For The Record

Never tell me again an angel
of your god, that nameless lover
of slit throats, burnt flesh,
stayed your hand. Do not insist
the hapless ram died in my place;
lost to desire, tangled in thorn,
he is more your totem than mine.
No covenant, no matter what
you tell yourself, requires our
bloody signatures; no sacrament
requires a knife. My mother's veil
you twisted and used to blind me
slipped: no one was there but us.

Villanelle

"You think you can walk right out?"
my father said. I did. I went
as far as I could from that house,

far from that town. I doubt
I could have traveled farther had I meant
to change my name, to walk right out

of the life I was born to, to applause
the world insists will make us confident
but never does. I trusted from that house

to this one, bridges burnt, the roads out,
even demons wouldn't dare, but hell-bent
quests are circles: storm right out,

a son hurt and rebellious,
and in half a lifetime, in bewilderment,
you come home to your own house

and your sullen son without
the evidence to prove you're innocent.
Some days I want to walk right out,
but can't, won't, must not leave this house.

Shouting Match With My Son

for Robert, age 14

If you knew how much it hurts
when I feel your fear of me,
how fast I am you and at once
my father, maybe you could see

escape, the hole in the fence,
the narrow break in the wall
that I, with more experience,
cannot, and barely recall.

I don't know why we're here
again, bewildered, jaw to jaw,
but I am finally clear:
this is a failure, not a law.

I am no Abraham. No monstrous
god, not even memory, demands
the repetition of what once was
done to me. These calloused hands,

dumb clubs of rage,
have held the same two nothings
since I was about your age.
Where are the winnings

manhood promised me?
Later. Tomorrow. The future.
Enough. Who I wanted to be
I am: your father, and you're

the future, facing me here,
where love, with all its tender
trust at risk, meets fear,
and to win we must surrender.

The Scientific Method

When you begin to feel the first tear well,
place the vial against the lower lid and,
gently, with the fingers of your other hand,
lift above the eye. Let the tear fall

by itself - don't touch it - in the vial.
It helps to do this in front of a mirror.
Remember: be honest if you make an error.
Naturalness and purity are essential.

Keep at least that one eye open wide.
Don't force the tear in any way.
Sometimes a tear won't come on a given day.
Make note of the fact that you tried

but couldn't cry, and then proceed.
You have a stopper and a coded label
for each vial. Are you comfortable?
You should have everything you need.

You see all tears are not the same.
Apply them to the neutral paper
and countless shades of color appear.
Our study is to give each hue a name.

2000

Finally, the deposition,
the 13th station.

Bring oil, clean linen.
Lay him in his grave.

Hell, two millennia's
enough for anyone.

What's left to save?

Let him go, he's done,
the bloody, obedient son.

Yet

Sounds East European, doesn't it?
Yet.
A town in the Urals, the western
border of Asia, where everyone hurries
calmly through the narrowest of streets
to rocky fields, hard, patched by snow so dry
it hurts. Yet
every single day they make their way there;
every night come back.

Yet.
The ring of an ancient Egyptian god.
An animal, probably like a musk-ox,
slowly dragging tomorrow from over the mountains;
(can a word be a god? can anything but
a word be a god? for us, I mean)
always and never arriving.

Umbilicus: Vision: Promise: Deadlock:
(the deciding vote has not been cast
yet) I, pharaoh by default, acknowledge you
most powerful of all. O lord of heads sometimes,
tails sometimes, lord of the other hand,
there is no escape from you
yet.

To My Children

to Robert and Veronica

A dog that sniffs a book
knows it as well
as I know this world;
that much I know.

Still, I try to make it
make some sense
without lying, but
the truth is I'm afraid

that by the time I find
the needle in the rick,
the knack, the trick, if
not an explanation, then
a way, if not a way, a
position, you'll be gone,

sojourning in your
own bewilderment, and I
will call the knowledge
I could tell you nothing
wisdom. Contradictions,

I will offer after you,
are aggravating
but the parts you need
to build the means
to go in both directions:
away from home and back.

Formula

If you bring your hands together
back to back, thumbs down,
the opposite of prayer,

between two moments, any two,
the way you might open the thighs
of a large and curious volume

and breathe deeply there,
you will be able to disappear,
but never do this

without first placing a name,
not your own, beneath your tongue
where the two veins meet

if you wish to return.

Same Time As Always

for Kathi

All day today I heard a voice. On the bus
Someone whispered my name in my ear.
Later, on the train, same thing.
I turned but no one was there.
I haven't been this nuts in years,
I thought. I wiped my face, afraid.
Now home same time as always,
I head upstairs. You call. I turn.
You smile. And then I know
The whole day long it was you. You.

Good Thing

The explanations and peptalks are facile.
Deaths and the death of love have left me weakened.
It's a damn good thing the heart's a muscle.

Because it's later and worse than it was, I'll
try again. After each loss, myths beckoned:
excuses, wishes, peptalks much too facile,

fancy-dancing, dreaming, backing from the easel,
from the portrait I sketched till I sickened.
It's a damn good thing the heart's a muscle,

not gray jelly like what wobbles in the skull
and looks for words; or bone that aches and
hardens, brittle as dogma, to a child's facile

stick-man. In the heart the will is gristle.
I or anyone I love could die at any second.
It's a damn good thing the heart's a muscle

that has no choice, that has to wrestle
with itself continually to live, a paradox and
proud of it, an old creed anything but facile,
a damn good dumb involuntary muscle.

Covenant

; then the god, the father, bit
the tip off the boy's.

"Tell," he warned,
"and I'll eat the rest. Here,
use these for bandages."

And from his black bag,
promises and dreams.

The artist of today becomes unreal if he remains in his ivory tower or sterilized if he spends his time galloping around the political arena. Yet between the two lies the arduous way of true art.

— Albert Camus

Six Paintings By Matisse

for Alberto de Lacerda

1. La Desserte Rouge, 1908

Who is this figure, busy, always, with
preparations, amid blood-red illusions,
guardian of the bold or boring heart?
Lub-dub. Big deal. Sit down. The tongue!
Now there's an organ fleshly, necessary
and orchestral as an artist's eye. Look,
there, through the window in the thick wall:
the wobbling world like a liquid's surface.
Now look at her: her look, meant to hide her,
gives her away — Mnemosyne, wise mother,
arranging the season's fruits and flowers.

2. La Fenetre, 1916

Even as we have arranged it,
the world goes on without us,
lives, breathes, moves, and changes,

not only because it is green (a word
that, much like "light," means more
than is ever intended) but because

what summons each new topography
from time's fatigue, cruel as it is,
(no, not to show us, but we notice)

leaves beauty in its wake, light
through a green that froths and vanishes
over and over and over.

3. La Danse II, 1909-1910

So much illusion in even a single moment:
from childhood's bedtime tigers in the curtains
to dead friends' faces in the crowded street.
I wonder if we ever know what's real.

What shall we do? Survivors, more and more
of what we call the world the world calls
memory. Each morning brings a simple story
that becomes incomprehensible by evening.

Is the danger real? Is death? Who wants to know?
Who wants to know if things are as they seem?
If the unmistakable angel came and offered you
lucidity, eternally, what would you do?

We dance! We choose, who know the cost of fact,
the grip of others' hands and the abandon
only possible when we are held like this,
our links explicit, simple choreography

from childhood all we want or need although
we each, alone, know otherwise. It's hard
to tell from here, from this one moment, if
the changing sky is growing bright or dimming,

so we dance to forget then turn and wheel
the other way toward remembering until
we know, together, it is time to turn again,
and someone stumbles, falls, becomes a story.

4. La Famille Du Peintre, 1911

No still life: he must live
with this arrangement of
the family furniture, and paint it.
The dead chose the fabric.

Did le Pere our painter pose them?
We stare through the proscenium.
Daughter, stage left, moves to foot:
feigning displeasure, "Papa, stop it!"

Madame, up right, with kerchief,
mutters, wishing to vanish, angered
by this trespass that, because she wed
Matisse, will go on forever,

while Masters Cain and Able,
in their prepubescence, slow
as red fish in a glass bowl,
contend, center, throughout.

The dead are in the pit, below
the angle of our vision, tuning.
Half our lives we wait and then
they're awful anyway, off-key,

each in a different time.
But never mind. Before us the living
make believe and we believe in them.
Vague sounds of war and weeping, off.

5. La Conversation, 1909-1911

This is "intercourse" the way the word is
used in older texts we giggled at in school.
He is phallos, a fluted column, a pillar,
composed in blue and white pajamas, serious,

while, folded and dark, she holds herself
a little stiffly, as if she's been interrupted
in her enjoyment of the morning's solitude,
but listening nonetheless. If it isn't obvious

from the sheer intensity of their locked gaze
in the electric blue interior, the iron restraint
on the sill of the warming world spells NOX,
and in its center familiar sleeping lovers lie,

turned from each other, curled, while outside,
day is already begun. They are discussing what to do,
where to go, how to get there, needs and wants,
love's fierce and difficult engagement.

6. L'Atelier Rouge, 1911

Only a dead man,
only a dead man here,

an absence limned
by what can be said

to exist, a familiar
array of records and effects,

life death the way all
shadows are the sun: a

Matisse.

The Backyard Stuff's Essential

after A. R. Ammons

There's a small hill in the tall grass in the backyard
that's a perfect pillow. Summer's my lazy time if lazy's
understood the way I mean it: wagging fingers, dirty

looks be damned. Implied utility's a constant
in a view, even up through birdshook foliage
or looking at clodhopping robins hunting worms,

spotting a split-second rabbit, or reflecting
on the house that costs so much to live in (nothing
much: 2BR, bath, eat-in kitch, den, lvng rm):

nice portion of an acre though and privacy preserved
by hemlock hedges, cedar, and rhododendron:
comfortable terrain around the nest: good sleeping.

Yet like everything else alive I have competitors
and predators (creditors): presently I carry a balance
due on several past accounts: their statements, in-

voices they call them, flimsy tissues, flush with alarm
at repercussions, service interruptions, spotty
ratings, garnishings, and heavy levies on extra time

and on my quietude. My neighbor's mower has the power
of a motorcycle and its hypertense demeanor, growling
at a distance, makes the stiff grass on my sweaty arms

stop itching: now it's a delicate tickle. Why do choices
seem to come in twos? I don't want to go anywhere
or do anything right now although a bright idea

might occur to me watching a squirrel in the oak
lie full-length on a limb and stretch out like a cat,
or staring into the effulgent redscape of my eyelids

(where the will is situated, surely) with the bright sun
free a while between the slowly counterearthwise clouds
and I'll get up and do it then or go there.

Stevens Astride The Hemispheres

for Thom Salmon

Mnemosyne upreared amid atrocity concurs:
this looking backward is a not so accidental
death and dismemberment policy after all,

appended to one's life and health; however,
squat caryatids, resentful though proud,
agree that, whether a bequest or metaphor

(those fixed, equivocating lions), history
is more than books and books of big stuff and
(roaring leonisimus or sleeping as you pass)

requires no notice in advance to change the plan.
Believe me, there are times, *semblable*,
when such rays are visible slanting through

our covenants and riders that a calendar
might just as well, for all the useless fear
it tries to ease with seasonal photos, be

that grove of birches, each benignly slashed to
individuality by no one, it depicts so earnestly.
You never know. You can't. But you may trust

it fits together, boy, without a physical exam,
harmoniously, though all seems otherwise,
and no one has ever been denied. Call now.

Ars Poetica

A poem should be impenetrable and mute
About United Fruit,

The bomb,
The news, the noose, the why, the wherefrom,

And silent as the stolen
Stelae the museums own —

Narratives, judgments, records,
Long careers for buzzards.

A poem should be able to kill time
As the Dow climbs,

Leaving, as the moon releases
Spire by spire the debt-entangled cities,

Leaving, as the moon behind the make believe
Reason by reason the mind —

A poem should be able to kill time
As the Dow climbs.

A poem should add up to
Not true.

For all the history of belief
A boozy tear and a gold fig leaf.

For love
A State Department memo and a gunboat on the sea.

A poem should not mean
But flee.

Note: Archibald MacLeish's *Ars Poetica* is familiar to readers as an advertisement for the aestheticist approach to poetry, dear to those who would exclude all social criticism and public speech from literature. It is often the only poem of MacLeish's included in anthologies. However, MacLeish went on to write powerful poems against fascism abroad and McCarthyism in the US. He published *Ars Poetica* in his first book, and appears to have written it when he was 19 or 20 years old.

Poem on my 53rd birthday

In another ten or fifteen years
when it comes time to get elegaic
about all we might have done,
I'll be a hell of a poet;
I'll break your fucking heart.
But these days I still want

the rich to remove their designer
boots from the necks of the poor;
I want us all to stop and think
what premises we hold as natural
though they were written down
by men who were *flawed*, as we say,

by which we mean that it pleased them
to exact the tribute for their blessing
by fucking our children. (I know,
because I've been to art school,
this is not a real poem; real poems only
find aims afterward and accidentally.

Please listen anyway, okay?)
I want the understanding that we have
been duped to lead us this time
not into shame but an angry questioning.
Music? You want music? Call Sousa,
call Nero. Hup!.. two, three, four;

I'm going to stop right here. No
hip hypno-lullabies, no verbal
origami. I have paid attention
some years in a row now and I know
which side I'm on. You with the jargon,
the excuses, the pardons, watch out.

We live in an occupied country, misunderstood;
Justice will take us millions of intricate moves.

— William Stafford

WTC NYC

1.

The planning, the precision, the devotion;
the crater a cathedral built toward hell.

Playing children making sounds of gunfire.
I am making myself reread Ecclesiastes.

The dead keep fertile our earthen hearts;
without them we are as dust as they.

In the quiet, the underside of the future,
beginnings call, drops of water in a clay pot.

We are going to have to live
a long time now to comprehend this sadness.

2.

We have words for things we've never seen
and things we've seen we have no words for.

Knowing how a clock works tells us
nothing of telling, or understanding, time.

The shadows of the generals on the maps
are shadows of the bombers on the land.

Wait! Wait! Wait a minute!
I thought we were only talking!

The goose-step again, the graves,
the furnaces, the mushroom cloud.

Of all the green plants there are few
that bring forth what we'd call a flower.

Hockshop

It's a window next to impossible
to miss unless
you're hurrying to a particular place
or obsessed with a recent song, or carrying
a face, not just anyone's,
with you at the time.

I confess I've stood there
under the sign lettered GUNS - JEWELRY – LOANS
many times, the window full of
risked, lost, or stolen things,
grieving people's or dead people's things,
novelties and knives.

Guilt. Indecision. Everything
is used; each of the hundreds of watches
shows a different time. Guitars,
untuned, hang carefully, gratefully
silent. Which ones, of these alarm clocks,
above the guns, above the stuffed owls,

have cut off a dream and sent a man out
to die? Some of these paintings,
stacked on the floor, have hung in the finest
banks, and, although it's kept quiet,
there are those who'll say the diamonds
were swept from the highway after a fatal crash

that no one remembers. Not even
the broker, the nodder, the blank-faced one
who asks no questions, who, come night,
empties the window, leaves the drawer open
and empty, leaves one light on, sighs,
locks up, drags shut the rusty gates.

Parting In Winter

1.

The hulk lurches, bucks, booms
forward gathering speed and I
glimpse her, on the platform,
waiting to go in the other direction;

poles flick over her faster then faster then
the black wall roars beside me
and I stare at myself thinking:
Me. My fault. My anger. Mine.

2.

The new apartment is empty, a box
painted white: the taste of chalk
in my mouth, the dry taste of fear:
a walk in deep snow, forks,
hooks, the cutter, scythes
rusting underneath.

Pieces of the ceiling lie around on the floor
where I sprawl nights, trying hard
to fill myself with what chairs,
lamps, tables, pictures will go where,

while outside, in the street, a woman sings,
and I go to the window, muscle it,
bang it, hang on it, it
won't close. Her song is cold.

3.

Thanksgiving: the feast an excuse
to gorge ourselves: the wishbone

between us, (the shape of a harness:
how did we come to be so small?)

each of us holding an end,
each of us with our wasted wish

for the bigger piece.
How did we come to be so small?

4.

    Failing, I could at least
tell you how under the
    slow stroking

    of your marks and signs,
under our potion
    of bellyfroth, I used

    every glide to hover,
all that was left of my powers,
    every eyelash trick

    to hold in the cove
the deafness won from
    the flume's roar;

    clutch, keep. The boat rocks,
even moaning, even
    calling me. Calling.

    And I wanted to say
what I believed I had
    learned and how

but my tongue must have
been dreaming, waking
    now, in its own bed

    far away. And far away and
totem to you now I am
    trying to untangle

    this distance from around
my legs so you can come
    here, where I wait

    and remember, fear
and forget, willing myself
    willing. Anxious.

Do Tell

I tell
you what:
you tell
me what
you want,
I tell
you what
I have.
I tell
you what
I want,
you tell
me what
you have.
We have
the time
to tell
each other
what we
want but
this time
we have
to tell
the truth.

"So What"

Here is a tiny weapon, devastating, undetectable.
Here is the switch to turn off the world.

The demise of an ancient question;
the voice no longer rises,

and a black hole, antimatter, widens
like a desperate pupil in the sudden dark.

Neruda: Ode To Money

for Olga Venegas

Green, valuable,
easy to waste,
hard to earn.
Need of the poor
who dare not hope for it
while the rich
don't know its real worth.
Money, a paper that tears
the brotherhood
each has a right to.
Money, the hope
to go on living,
this green ticket
not all want to share.
Money. Money. Money.
Just because I go on
wanting you
does not mean I am content
to go on needing you
until you kill me.

The Buddy System

"It is hard to have friends now. People
are going to pieces too fast. They hate
anyone who does not bleed fog and sickness."

— Kenneth Patchen

I'm down. I go to see him.
I show him the teeth I broke on what I thought
were breasts. I show him my empty wallet.
He says what I expect, "Just rest, relax,
you did your best. You want to talk about it?"

Pulling off my boots I think
how all my friends, at one time or another, tell me
what weird friends I have. "I have to have
weird friends" I tell them, "what's a stranger
life than a circle of mirrors? What is lonelier?"

He tries, my friend. He plops banal
analogies in a bowl, a mush, a grits
eucharist: the fallow field, the greatest hitters'
greatest slumps. I eat it up and wash it down
with cheap red wine from a gallon jug.

Both of us are very thirsty. Soon
we're bleeding drunken laughter that abruptly
clots. Our eyes meet. Both of us
feel weird. "It's late." "I know."
"I'd better go. Hey, listen... thanks."

"Oh what are friends for, anyway?"
The door is open now. I think that friends are for
this groggy warmth from which we see more
soberly our limits. Outside the fog lends
phony haloes to the ordinary lights.

The New Life

A new love is a new life. I arrive
and just inside your door (my melting coat
you take and throw somewhere)
put down my suitcase (full of holes
so that the monkey off my back I
stuffed inside can breathe) pull off my shoes
and standing in the ice-cold puddle
take you in my arms and give you goosebumps.

It's decided: we will find a garden
apartment, furnish it with odds and ends
(the odds are steep as the rent, our ends
are loose and sometimes meet) and slowly
summon, as we need it, patience
out of passion. You will meet my monkey
(love me love my nephew) with his repertoire
of funky smells, a screech per memory, and pranks.

I'm living serious — there *is* a difference: love
knocked neither of us down. Epithalamions
this tongue-in-cheek (my tongue in yours
and yours in mine) are frowned on, suspect.
This, however, is for you, aware a new love
lives on clarity and laughter and a new life
is impossible. Let's put the table over by the window.

Above The Falls

Watch them on the footbridge
above the falls
that keeps us from hearing what they say:
he leans on the lake side, looking far across,
she, above the falls, looks down.

We can imagine what he sees
is moving with the water to the falls.
that the reflections of the trees, the clouds,
the docks and houses are a swirling
surface-film distorted as it

pours, silken, over the lip. Or
we can decide she feels the colors
bleed from everything behind her,
and that the brittle pieces of it
crash, continuously, at her feet

like an infinite stack of dishes.
He's crossing to her now, his arms
around her from behind, his
fingers buckled at her waist. Look:
when she turns to him

he turns his eyes away
as if he'd begun to blurt the truth
then clapped a hand to his mouth.
She touches him dishonestly and gently.
We can imagine reasons

why they do not love each other
anymore; we can infer,
by their doubling back
the way they came, the touchy
mutual denial their conversation

had to steer around
to stay together one more day,
but neither of us, even now, knows
anything that either one of them can say
to make things right again.

What It Takes

The cuckoo in the dark
alone, takes fifty-nine
minutes to prepare.

Loss

I wake still tired
with all of me numb,
a limb I've slept on.

I'm raw to the salt
and pepper shakers,
figures on a wedding cake.

Your chair is empty
so I sit in it
and stare at mine.

The mirror often, but
your name on pills, your razor,
never hurt before.

When I make the bed,
I punch the pillows together
and cover your body.

From A Front Window

1.
There is the city of glass and money,
over there, but here it comes,
closer with every newspaper.
Unidentified lying spokesmen
interpret the same old photos:
the bloody feet of refugees,
the bloody hands of soldiers.
Here comes someone, not a neighbor,
with a clipboard and a calculator.
Where will we grow children and roses?
Where will we grow older?

2.
Because mothers still tell children
making ugly faces to be careful
or they will harden into one of them,
I am a little less afraid.

When fathers wipe their children's dirty faces
with handkerchiefs that smell of sweat,
their children do not forget them
easily. I am a gladdened father
learning that, and a calmer son.

3.
And lovers' bodies make a clumsy knot
just good enough to mend the net.

You'll Never Know What Hit You

The sailor returns with the map filled in.

In a vain attempt to save the dragon
industry, churches begin to preach
appreciation for the metaphorical.

Soon calendars become the thing.
As far as planning, the populace
is mostly on its own, the future
even stranger now that it's foreseeable.

Personal agency, good works and all that,
on the ropes since well before the Inquisition,
makes a comeback. "To do" lists abound.

Taxes, of course, go up, a little larger
piece of each day lopped off like a heel
of bread as tribute to the cartoon on the coin,
the face of the man who trades the sailor fame
for silence, who pays the minstrels he calls
poets to sing jingles for cartographers.

Stop! You want to shout. Just stop! Is this,
this residue of avarice what we intended?
A few more licks at the last salty
continents with bleeding tongues? The world
is not diminished, not made smaller, not now
comprehensible, nor ever will be. Stop!

A rock, a rubber bullet, a dum-dum, a truncheon,
a shoe, a two-by-four, a pipe upside your head.

Table For Two

You raise an eyebrow and nod.
I'm going on and on about how next time
but you're elsewhere, as if hearing,

on an old tape, old music, voices,
young ones, ours; the screech of a chair
and your old footsteps coming closer, louder...

You look at me as if you've just awakened;
as if the people we used to be turned off
the switch. Do you blame them?

Jove's Moon

from NASA text

Lacking sufficient gravity, Eros
has always made close approaches
a delicate challenge for controllers;

for example, the NEAR spacecraft,
unmanned, is now its satellite.
Attempts to ascertain its shape

amount to successive approximations.
Only one of the group called Amors, ·
its surface is cratered by chance collisions.

While repeated imaging has refined knowledge,
fly-by observations have not provided answers.
We do not have sufficient information.

Poor Freud,

"Freud's theory of sexuality was the half-truth with which he reconfigured his own traumas and anxiety."

— Louis Breger, FREUD: DARKNESS IN THE MIDST OF VISION

walking home,
clips a cigar,
wants nothing much:
an evening's peace,
some coke in the vein,
a postulate to chew on;
maybe he will finally
write that letter
to his father. But
they come again:
the boys like monkeys
chattering around him
waving handguns;
the girls bent over,
wiggling their asses.
Where to turn? How
to fly? They trample
him, a wet leaf
plastered to the century,
his flat, stern visage
trembling on the sidewalk
like a paper dollar.

American Sign

Your house,
on fire!

On fire!

They will
not
hear.

Your house!
On fire!

Their lips say
O
beautiful.
O
such

exquisite
gestures.

The Definite Article

The people crowded the square.
The crowd peopled the square.
The troops circled the square.
The troops and the people squared off.

The name of the people is they.
The name of the troops is not us.
The name of the square is there.
The name of the circle is again.

The square peopled the news.
The news circled the world.
The troops circled the crowd.
The world turned the page.

The name of the news is yesterday.
The name of the paper of course.
The name of the new page is maybe.
The name of the world is asleep.

Failed Apostrophe

Can a poet still talk to a bird
and answer as a bird and
ask a question that itself is
a bird that flashes through
foliage, green leaves falling?
I know what birds think,
I think. I know what they say:
Mine. You stay away.
Stay away, stay away, stay away.

But this morning, half-asleep and
bending for the paper, one hand
holding shut my robe, I hear
back to a small backyard,
two boys, dead brothers, digging
in fragrant dirt, our mother, also
gone, calling to come inside while
the unintentioned birds, knowing
nothing of death, are singing:
You're okay, you're okay, you're okay.

Ghazal

Spare us from men who believe in another world.
Save us from men who only believe in this world.

Look at the thief, the murderer, the rapist getting away!
The world is his, the one he believes in, this world.

The martyr's myth-enchanted mind and mumbling lips
and every atom of him gone. See? Believe in this world.

Can we please return to the theme of romantic love?
The killers called it womanly, our belief in this world.

There must be a place where lovers never part and yet
one must be in love and lonely to believe in this world.

I ought to know. I've seen both enemies and lovers die.
I ought to but don't see how to be alive in this world.

Clear

Believe in this water come
from deep earth high
clouds answer and question
curse and blessing from
seas and rivers through
sluices over falls down
spouts through pipes in
buckets pitchers cups or
not still it will
slake your thirst.

Forgiveness

Apart from both the certainty of maps
and the panic at being suddenly lost

is an open place, like a great square
in an ancient city of winding streets.

You know it. Once or twice we've found it
just when we were about to give up.

If we're separated, for whatever reason,
and you find it first, wait there for me.

Whatever you do, don't double back.
And if I find it first, I'll wait for you.

Cedar Hill Publications

SET THIS BOOK ON FIRE!—*Jimmy Santiago Baca*
$15—Poetry ISBN: 1-891812-23-8

THE HEAT: *Steelworker Lives and Legends*
$15—Prose & Poetry ISBN: 1-891812-17-3

AMNESIA TANGO—*Alan Britt*
$10—Poetry ISBN: 1-891812-14-9

AMERICAN MINOTAUR—*Leonard J. Cirino*
$9—Poetry ISBN: 1-891812-22-X

96 SONNETS FACING CONVICTION—*Leonard J. Cirino*
$10—Poetry ISBN: 1-891812-20-3

THE TERRIBLE WILDERNESS OF SELF—*Leonard J. Cirino*
$10—Poetry ISBN:1-891812-00-9

the despairs—*Cid Corman*
$15—Poetry ISBN: 1-891812-30-0

INFINITIES—*Lucille Lang Day*
$15—Poetry ISBN: 1-891812-31-9

SUBURBAN LIGHT—*William Doreski*
$10—Poetry ISBN: 1-891812-16-5

BODY AND SOUL—*Sharon Doubiago*
$15—Poetry ISBN: 1-891812-24-6

THE SILK AT HER THROAT—*James Doyle*
$10—Poetry ISBN: 1-891812-12-4

NEXT EXIT—*Taylor Graham*
$10—Poetry ISBN: 1-891812-13-0

BEYOND RENEWAL—*George Held*
$10—Poetry ISBN: 1-891812-29-7

THE CROWD OF TIME—*Timothy Hodor*
$15—Poetry ISBN: 1-891812-41-6

WITHOUT PARADISE—*Richard Hoffman*
$15—Poetry ISBN: 1-891812-33-5

7th CIRCLE—*Maggie Jaffe*
$10—Poetry ISBN: 1-891812-07-6

THE PRISONS—*Maggie Jaffe*
$15—Poetry ISBN: 1-891812-21-1

SHADOW OF THE PLUM—*Carol Lem*
$15—Poetry ISBN: 1-891812-32-7

WHITHER AMERICAN POETRY—*Michael McIrvin*
$14—Critical Essays ISBN: 1-891812-26-2

THE BOOK OF ALLEGORY—*Michael McIrvin*
$10—Poetry ISBN:1-891812-03-3

PROVERBS FOR THE INITIATED—*Kenn Mitchell*
$11—Poetry ISBN: 1-891812-06-8

1917—*Joe Napora*
$10—Poetry ISBN: 1-891812-18-1

BRAMBLECROWN—*Georgette Perry*
$5—Poetry ISBN: 1-891812-25-4

GRAY AIR—*Christopher Presfield*
$8—Poetry ISBN: 1-891812-15-7

GUTTERSNIPE CANTICLE—*Amelia Raymond*
$9—Poetry ISBN: 1-891812-22-X

"EDEN, OVER . . ."—*Tim Scannell*
$5—Poetry ISBN:1-891812-01-7

routine contaminations—*Deborah Small*
$15—Art & Prose ISBN: 1-891812-09-2

SOME SORT OF JOY—*John Taylor*
$15—Prose ISBN: 1-891812-08-4

THE WORLD AS IT IS—*John Taylor*
$15—Prose ISBN: 1-891812-04-1

KID WITH GRAY EYES—*Mark Terrill*
$10—Poetry ISBN: 1-891812-28-9

AMERIKA / AMERICA—*Marilyn Zuckerman*
$15—Poetry ISBN: 891812-40-8

PIECES OF EIGHT: *A Women's Anthology of Verse*
$10—Poetry ISBN:1-891812-02-5

JAM: *Cedar Hill Anthology Series*
$10—Poetry ISBN: 1-891812-05-X